Officers in the major incident control unit draw up an emergency plan

The most serious fire in Banstead in anyone's memory occurred on the night of Friday 12th December 2008. Waitrose supermarket, in the High Street, was engulfed in flames after a fire started in the roof soon after 8.30pm. Soon, the blaze was so fierce that windows of shops on the opposite side of the main road exploded in the heat. Dozens of families were evacuated to church halls as 100 firefighters from all over Surrey and South London tackled the inferno. Surrey Mirror chief photographer Keith Walter was at the scene and captured on camera these dramatic images.

Police officers warn a group of inquisitive teenagers to stay away from the scene

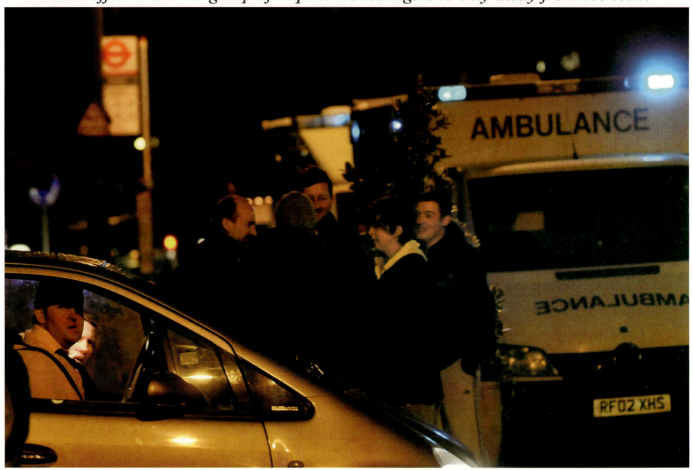
Friends gather near the Woolpack public house to talk excitedly of the drama

The fire takes hold and within minutes has ravaged through the supermarket

The flames spread with alarming rapidity, threatening nearby homes and shops

The December night sky is illuminated by the ferocious flames

A security camera alongside Avenue Road alerted police to the roof blaze

The framework of the blazing buildings can be seen in a brief clearing of the smoke

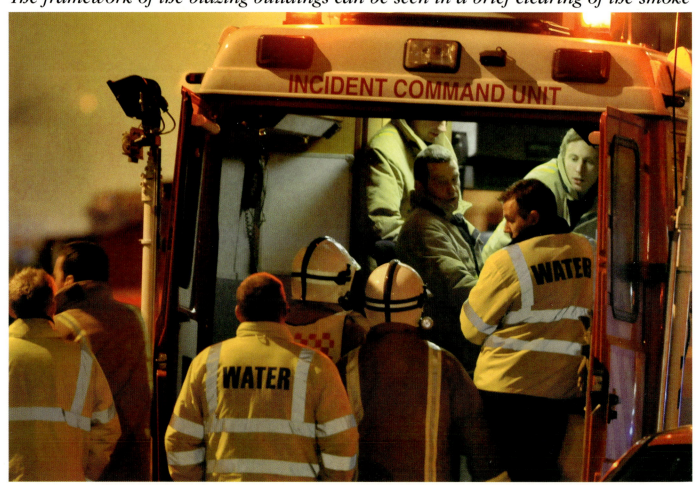
The incident command unit team brief the emergency services

Fire crews using a hyraudlic platform play water onto the inferno

Children's swings in the recreation ground silhouetted against the fire

'Get out of the restaurant now!'

DINERS enjoying an evening meal in one Banstead restaurant were among those led to safety. Among the customers in the Royal China, High Street, was Michael Selby, a resident of Nork for nearly 30 years and a community leader. Councillor Selby, who represents Nork Residents' Association on Reigate and Banstead Council recalled: "We could smell burning and thought the fumes were coming from the kitchen. When we looked out of the window we thought it was snowing but then we realised it was ash coming down and saw the supermarket on fire.

"We saw the fire brigade arrive and were watching it all when suddenly, without warning, there was a massive explosion."

It was reported by Banstead's MP Crispin Blunt that a gas cylinder had exploded and sent roof tiles flying more than 100 yards, shattering shop windows opposite. Four firefighters were said to have suffered minor injuries.

Councillor Michael Selby – led to safety

Mr Selby said: "The police went into the restaurant and told the management to escort us out quickly through the back door. I had no time to collect my coat.

"We walked along an alleyway holding hands, like a human chain. What was terrifying was the acrid smoke we were inhaling. Many of us were finding it hard to breathe. It was absolutely shocking. We were lucky the windows didn't blow in."

Mr Selby, who served as an electrical engineer in the Merchant Navy and worked for 20 years for Lloyds Bank in the City, was not the only local resident caught up in the drama.

When Laura Trotman looked out of a window at her home in Park View, Avenue Road, she witnessed a scene "like the pictures of the Great Fire of London."

Residents of Avenue Road described seeing the sky orange with the flames leaping out of the building.

Rosie Tickle, 17, a bakery assistant, told a newspaper reporter that she was working at the store when the fire started.

"We were evacuated and went to the car park and we saw black smoke and then the flames.

"It feels surreal that it all burnt down, because when we were evacuated we did not think the fire was going to be that big."

Another member of staff said he finished his shift an hour previously. He lived down the road and felt the explosion.

As the evacuation of 60 residents took place and the Baptist Church hall filled, there were concerns that the hall itself was too near the inferno.

Borough Council leader Joan Spiers reported that the council was asked to support the emergency services' efforts by opening a rest centre for 60 local residents evacuated from their homes.

In collaboration with Surrey County Council's social services, the Banstead Centre was used and 42 people spent the night there in safety.

Flames leap from the roof as Councillor Selby is led to safety with other diners

The Royal China and neighbouring shops

At the height of the blaze, some 60 firefighters were engaged in quelling the flames

Challenge for the fire brigade

THIRTY people phoned 999 to report the initial outbreak of fire at Waitrose. Among the first calls to the Surrey Fire and Rescue's control centre at Reigate was one from Surrey Police, who had seen images of the supermarket's roof fire on a CCTV camera just yards away. The first of the calls was made at 8.36pm and crews from Epsom fire station were summoned to the scene. Although the crews entered the burning building wearing breathing apparatus, they were soon withdrawn for their own safety.

At 8.52pm, after making a swift assessment of the rapidly spreading fire, the Epsom firefighters radioed the control room with the urgent request: "Make pumps four". The help of a brigade aerial ladder platform – a type of turntable ladder – was also sought and this was despatched from Chertsey. But the extra fire engines were soon deemed to be insufficient to deal with the severity of the blaze and a further "SOS" message of "make pumps six" was sent from Banstead at 9.17pm. An additional aerial platform ladder was also requested.

Just three minutes later, the control room took yet another alarming message from the first fire crews at Waitrose: "Make pumps 10". This indicated to the control staff how grave the situation was and a full emergency procedure was initiated.

Over the next few hours, fire engines were drafted in from far and wide – not just from Surrey's own stations but from London Fire Brigade, too. Among the London fire stations which sent crews were Purley, Sutton, Croydon, Wallington and Surbiton. Surrey's own firefighters from Epsom, Reigate, Guildford, Esher, Godstone, Painshill, Staines, Camberley, Walton on Thames and Oxted were all engaged in the fire-fighting operation throughout the night. A water tanker was also brought in from Dorking.

The incident commander, group manager Martin Riddle, said crews were faced with "a very serious fire in a highly populated place" and that the initial priority was to look after the safety of the surrounding community and the safety of the firefighters.

"I feel that we were successful," said Mr Riddle, looking back at the incident two months later. "We had to make the decision to rapidly evacuate people from the flats and houses nearest to the fire. The fire was taking a direct blast from the wind so we sprayed a wall of water between the supermarket and the neighbouring properties to thin the heavy smoke that was drifting across. This helped to wash down any burning material and sparks, too."

With the help of London Fire Brigade, Surrey Police and ambulance crews, the evacuation of properties was carried out. Mr Riddle said he was most appreciative of the assistance afforded by the minister of the Baptist Church [Rev Dr Paul Adams] who provided accommodation in the church hall.

"It was very windy and there was torrential rain. There were a lot of seriously wet people around and to be able to go somewhere dry was very helpful."

Station manager Steve Schooling officially declared the fire under control at 11.35am on the Saturday morning. The 200 x 130ft supermarket was "100 per cent destroyed."

Mr Riddle, speaking in February 2009, said he was not able to discuss any possible cause of the intense fire. And regarding the explosion, he said there were a number of factors that could have led to the blast.

The great fire as seen from Avenue

d at the height of the conflagration

The shell of the supermarket was still smouldering next morning

The fire-ravaged Waitrose building in the cold light of next day

Fire brigade officials arrive to assess the magnitude of the destruction

Villagers are faced with a High Street which is largely cordoned off next day

Great community spirit

THE vicar of Banstead and his family were particularly looking forward to Christmas in December 2008. Reverend David Chance was trying out an experiment to beautify All Saints' Church for the festive season by introducing a Christmas Tree Festival for the first time.

He had seen a similar celebration at a church in Ramsgate, Kent, and wondered if it would work in Banstead.

To get the ball rolling, the Clarke family in Croydon Lane nurtured 21 potted firs for the event. They were carefully moved into the ancient church off the High Street on Thursday 11th December by Mr Chance with the assistance of Margaret and Rod McFarlane, congregation members from High View, Cheam.

On the following day, just hours before the Great Fire, they were lovingly decorated by worshippers in readiness for the services over the Christmas season. Mr Chance said the peaceful village of Banstead was then shattered by the explosion and fire at Waitrose that same night.

"Was it like this when the Nazi bombs fell on Forge Steading and the Woolpack?," he thought.

Mr Chance was referring to the immense damage caused just before 9am on 8th August 1944 when a flying bomb, or doodlebug, fell near the eastern end of the High Street, killing an off-duty soldier, injuring 32 people and shattering the old Woolpack public house and The Forge next door and damaging at least two dozen homes and shops. Some 200 villagers were rendered homeless and were given food in the British Restaurant. The Woolpack was replaced by a modern public house building after this.

On the night of the Waitrose blaze, Mr Chance said his family's most major concern was for the safety of those living near the inferno.

Mr Chance's wife, Andrea, manned the phone at the Vicarage in Court Road with the help of their daughter, Lydia, while Miriam, another daughter, helped her father open the Institute next to All Saints' for any refugees and police officers.

Of particular concern was the welfare of the All Saints' honorary priest, the Reverend Patricia Westbrook, who having returned to her home in Glenfield Road that afternoon after an operation, was one of those evacuated because the police station end of the High Street was enveloped in billowing smoke.

Mr Chance recalled: "We searched for her at the police station, which was full of police from outside the area who had no idea where anything was in the village. So we told them our Church Hall was open.

"Then we called at the Baptist Church, which was filling with evacuees, but we couldn't find Pat. We couldn't cross the High Street, but contacted her by text on her mobile phone, and discovered she was spending the night with kind neighbours.

"Returning to the Institute we were joined by our churchwarden, Dennis Fox.

"We stood in the street watching great flaming chunks of the supermarket collapsing into the road,

The Reverend David Chance, vicar of Banstead, pictured at the May Queen festival in the All Saints' orchard in May 2008

while we braced ourselves for terrible news of casualties.

"Lydia, who works in accident and emergency at Epsom Hospital was especially worried."

Welcome news there were no casualties

Mr Chance said that gradually the news filtered through that miraculously no one was hurt in the night's dramatic events. "Thank God!"

"And we continued to thank God next morning. This should have been our happy united carol singing in the Church Orchard. I had invited Mrs Sarah Goad, Lord Lieutenant of Surrey, to come and join us and then to open the Christmas Tree Festival. She insisted on coming, to give us encouragement.

"A great storm broke over us, but the High Street traders encouraged us to sing our carols. So we hud-

# of Banstead's villagers

dled inside the church, with the door open facing the street, singing for our storm-struck and blackened village.

"On the Sunday we were still shell-shocked. Police allowed us to visit Pat, who had returned home. In church we prayed in thankfulness that no one was hurt, for the care and attention of the fire and police services and for the Waitrose staff.

"In the week that followed, queues of cars filed past the ruin as people took photos. Nothing had survived as the fire had spread very rapidly and all that was left was a mass of twisted metal and walling.

"But also that week, our schools came to church for their carol services, to give thanks, to see the trees and to offer money for the children of St James' schools in Lesotho.

"Leaders of the Banstead Five Churches met with our Baptist minister [Rev Dr Paul Adams] to pray, plan and offer support to the Waitrose managers and people. They thanked us for all the community's support. "The 12th December 2008 will be one of those defining moments in our village history."

The Reverend Dr Paul Adams, minister of Banstead Baptist church, who helped look after evacuees

Ninety evacuees

FULFILLING the covenant of the land on which Banstead Baptist Church is built, the Rev Dr Paul Adams threw open the doors for all those seeking respite from the fire, *writes Patsy Payne*. He was relaxing at home waiting for his wife to return on that freezing Friday night, when he heard a loud clunk he thought was his front door. But it wasn't – just the boom of an explosion from Waitrose reverberating through houses near to the High Street church.

He explained: "Soon after, I had a call from one of my mission apprentices to say that Waitrose was on fire.

"He was very concerned about one vulnerable person he knew who lived in premises near to Waitrose and he was having difficulty in gaining access. I grabbed my coat and camera and ran across the park towards the blaze to help. But while we tried to gain access to the flat, a strong south westerly wind fanned the flames to greater heights."

Dr Adams was trying to ascertain if the resident was actually in her home when he heard that his pastoral administrator and church key-holder Nigel Sewell had been asked by police if the church could be opened up to take in those evacuated from nearby houses and the flats above the shops.

While scores of firefighters battled the blaze, Dr Adams ran back to the church where he was joined by his wife and three other staff members, welcoming evacuees, firefighters, police and paramedics into the warmth of the large main auditorium.

On Friday evenings the church has lots of activities for young people finishing at 8.30pm. The fire started just after that time so all escaped the danger of walking past the blazing supermarket.

"It was an absolute miracle," said Dr Adams.

He and the helpers served tea and biscuits, soft drinks and sympathy to the evacuees who sat around in little groups. A number of them were shocked and at one time there were some 90 being taken care of here.

"There was a very subdued mood in the church. Some people were upset and disorientated. We served more that 300 cups of tea and coffee and sought to comfort and reassure them.

"And then there were children, so we got toys from the crèche and they appeared to have a good time," he added.

'A good time to come to the church' says the notice board at Banstead Baptist Church as firemen utilise the centre

There was also a small collection of dogs. "We put a large bowl of water down for them, but they sloshed it everywhere! So we put mats under the bowl and kept topping up the water."

One lady was most concerned because her dog was still stuck in her home near the blaze, but good-hearted friends and the police soon reunited the pair in the church.

"I think we had five dogs in here at one time," said Dr Adams.

They also had police and dozens of the brave firemen who very politely asked if they should take their boots off before entering the building for refreshment."

Dr Adams smiled:" I hadn't realised that their uniforms are not waterproof so some of them were drenched and absolutely freezing as the fierce wind blew the water back on them."

By 11.30pm, when police had interviewed many of the evacuees to see if they could tell them anything about the fire, a coach was arranged to take those unable to stay with friends, to the Community Centre in The Horseshoe where blankets and camp beds were at the ready. But that was only the end of the beginning for the church, with Dr Adams and his team staying up throughout the night and joined by other church members until 5pm on Saturday, continuing to act as a respite centre for the emergency services. Having been up and on the go for approximately 36 hours, he modestly said:"It's what you do isn't it?

"It was a privilege for this church to be used as an evacuation centre. We were glad to be involved because that's what we're about."

Interestingly, the land on which the church is built was once known as Pound Field where a century or so ago, lost sheep would be brought for eventual reclamation by their owner.

In 1896 the land was bought by four Christians concerned for the welfare of farm workers and servants in wealthy Banstead's big houses.

At that time a covenant was put on the land that it be used for nondenominational gospel mission work.

"We welcome anybody here in the name of Jesus, as the sign says over our front door, and that is just what we did," smiled Rev Adams.

Publication details

**Published by Mark Davison
North Bank, Smoke Lane, Reigate, Surrey
RH2 7HJ. Tel 01737 221215
e-mail: mark.davison1@virgin.net
March 2009
Copyright: Mark Davison/ East Surrey and Sussex News and Media, Reigate.
Mark Davison is the author of several local history books including** *Surrey in the Hurricane*, *Surrey in the Sixties* **and** *Surrey in the Seventies*.

**Editorial contributions from Patsy Payne, Neville Wilson, Jo Charlton, Holly Thompson.
Epsom Post, Surrey Mirror, All Saints' parish magazine, Banstead, and Surrey Comet. Additional photographs by Peter Gardner, Rev Dr Paul Adams, Phil Lee and Mark Davison.
Printed by Litho Techniques (Kenley) Ltd, Godstone Road, Whyteleafe, Surrey.
Front cover photograph by Keith Walter. Back cover by Rev Dr
Paul Adams.**

Surrey Mirror photographer Keith Walter took most of the fire pictures in this booklet

Rev Dr Paul Adams photographed these firemen in his Baptist church refuge

Steve on leave as store blazes

Steve Hilsley back at work in the temporary Waitrose store at the former Woolworth's. Immediately after the fire, Banstead's 205 employees were transferred to nearby branches in Epsom, Surbiton, New Malden, Worcester Park, Cobham and Hersham.

A WAITROSE employee at Banstead returned home from half a year's leave to discover his place of work no longer existed. Steve Hilsley, a manager at the Banstead branch, was celebrating 25 years' service with six months' paid leave when the store was destroyed by fire.

He said later: "When somebody told me the supermarket had burned down, I thought they were joking. When I came down to see it for myself, my jaw dropped in disbelief. It's difficult to explain how I felt."

An artist's impression of the planned new Waitrose store to replace the gutted premises went on show to the public at the URC Church, Banstead, in January 2009. Some 500 people turned up to the exhibition.

Historical notes

● In 1838, a village school was built at the corner of High Street and what became Avenue Road.

● In 1970, Waitrose takes over a block of shops and offices at Wingfield House at the western end of the High Street.

● In 1990, the village school moves to The Horseshoe and Waitrose builds a major new store on the school site and relocates from the other end of the High Street.

● On 12th December 2008, a huge blaze destroys the Waitrose store. Villagers began to talk of the event as "12/12".

● In January 2009, plans for a new store are shown to the public at a display in Banstead's United Reformed Church.

● On 12th February 2009, Waitrose moves into a temporary home in the former Woolworth's store, vacated just weeks earlier.

Woolworth's, 46 High Street, closed for business in January 2009

Temporary home in Woolworth's

Waitrose re-opens in a temporary home – the Woolworth's store, in High Street

Stuart Thompson, manager of Waitrose, Banstead, for 10 years, in the temporary store opened in Woolworth's

With amazing speed, the former Woolworth's store has been converted to a temporary Waitrose supermarket

BANSTEAD's Woolworth's store served its last shoppers in early January 2009. The chain was closed nationally after it was put into administrators' hands months earlier. A major discount sale attracted crowds to the Banstead store in December. Days later the shop was closed and stripped out. But with great speed, talks between the administrators and Waitrose led to a decision to convert the premises into a temporary home for the stricken Waitrose and shoppers greeted the news.

Shoppers praise move into Woolies

Dennis Brown

Kenneth Saunders

Amanda Love

Tracy Lovell

Stuart Thompson

Woolies in 2008

BANSTEAD's shoppers took kindly to the opening up of a temporary Waitrose store in the village following the great fire. The doors to the former Woolworth's store opened on 12th February 2009 and staff handed customers chocolates as they browsed.

Stuart Thomspon, manager of Waitrose, Banstead, for the past 10 years, was delighted with the reaction from shoppers. He said that the turnaround in just eight weeks was "absolutely phenomenal." He added that to see the previous store on fire was "absolutely devastating".

"It was such an emotional situation for everyone. This place goes beyond being just my place of work. It was horrendous to see it burning like that."
He said at the opening: "The response from customers has been amazing."

Although only a quarter the size of the destroyed store, people could "pretty well do their weekly shop here." There was no space or power facilities for frozen food and before wine or beer could be sold a licence would have to be obtained from the borough council.

Shopper Amanda Love, 35, of High Street, Banstead, said: "It's very compact but it's nice to have it back in the High Street and it's easy to push a buggy around in."

Dennis Brown, 72, of Holly Lane, Banstead, said he was relieved the store was back and joked that he hadn't eaten properly since Christmas.

Tracy Lovell, 52, of Nork, said it was wonderful Waitrose had returned.

Kenneth Saunders, 80, of Epsom Downs, was also among the first shoppers to visit the temporary store.

He said: "I think they've done very well to get it done in the short time they have. There were a few frozen things we couldn't get, but apart from that, we've managed to do the whole weekly shop."

The night we shall never forget..

The severity of the fire is demonstrated in this picture by Rev Dr Paul Adams

DOZENS of shocked villagers were evacuated from their homes as flames leapt from the blazing Waitrose supermarket. About 60 people from nearby homes were led through thick smoke to Banstead Baptist Church in the High Street.

The church's minister, Rev Dr Paul Adams, 61, said afterwards: "There was a very subdued mood in the church. People were upset and disorientated. We served more than 300 cups of tea and coffee and tried to keep the spirits up."

Ceila Lodge, 69, was evacuated along with her 73-year-old husband Keith and daughter, Christine, 43. The grandmother-of-two, of Glenfield Road, said: "I was watching television and could smell what I thought was a bonfire. We went out to the conservatory, then there was a terrific explosion which shook the windows. We could see flames over the top of the shops.

"At about 10pm, we had a knock on the door. It was the police, who took us to the bottom of the road and led us to the church."

Residents were moved to Banstead Community Centre in The Horseshoe as concerns about a second explosion grew.

Mrs Lodge said: "At about 12.30am, a bus arrived to take us to the community centre. They provided mattresses for people to sleep on. I did lie down but didn't manage much sleep."

Some residents were allowed home from 6.30am and most were back by 9.45am.

Grandfather-of-two, Desmond Churchman, 73, of Glenfield Road, said: "It went off like a bomb. We had to spend the evening at my daughter's house."

Alfred Dodd, 83, and his wife, Josephine, 69, spent the evening at his step-son's home in Cheam.

Mr Churchman said: "We were at home and heard the explosion. At first we thought it must have been someone letting off a firework outside.

"My wife and I used to shop at the store. It's so sad this close to Christmas."

Paul Duffy, who was with his brother, Michael, on the High Street, said: "We just heard this massive bang. Everyone was saying 'get down, get down.' We didn't know what it was. It was pretty shocking."

Shocked Waitrose staff said they rallied outside the supermarket minutes before the explosion.

One 18-year-old delicatessen worker said: "We were getting ready to close when the alarm went off. People asked the managers if it was a false alarm, but they said it wasn't.

"When we met outside and could see the flames, black smoke was everywhere. We were moved by firemen down the road. After the explosion, people started crying. Everyone was in shock."

Another Waitrose worker described a huge ball of black smoke which suddenly billowed from the building before the blast.

She said: "I called my dad who came to pick me up. When we got home we heard this huge bang. We just looked at each other and thought, Oh my God! It was completely terrifying."

Former worker Kate Bowells, 61, from Carshalton, worked at the store for six years and described it as "the heart of the community." The mother-of-two said: "I just can't believe what's happened. The shop was a real meeting place for people in the area, expecially the elderly.

"It was so sad to see the Christmas tree hanging out of the upstairs window."